For Val

PORTRAIT OI

A year with the wildlife of Christchurch Park

Written and illustrated by
Reg Snook

Edited by
Ann Snook and Richard Wilson

Gresham

Reg Snook

First Published in 2011 by Gresham Publications in
association with
The Friends of Christchurch Park, Ipswich

www.focp.org.uk

Text © 2011 Reg Snook
Illustrations © 2011 Reg Snook

*A catalogue record of this book is available from
the British Library*

Snook, Reg
Portrait of a Park/Reg Snook

Printed by Tuddenham Press Ltd.

ISBN 978-0-9561080-1-2

CONTENTS

ACKNOWLEDGEMENTS

These wildlife notes began three years ago as fortnightly, hand-written 'jottings' on the Friends of Christchurch Park's notice board in Ipswich. I should like to thank the following for helping to turn those notes into this book: Philip Murphy for his ornithological expertise; Ann Snook for her support and her considerable typing skills; Peter Howard-Dobson for his assistance on the finer points of publishing; Richard Wilson for his time and enthusiasm in helping bring the book to print; and of course Mabel, who has lightened up the lives of so many!

INTRODUCTION

This book is a collection of fortnightly articles that were originally posted on the notice board of the Friends of Christchurch Park next to the Reg Driver Visitor Centre in the Park. Arranged here roughly in chronological order beginning and ending in winter, they are designed to give the general reader an idea of what is happening to the Park's wildlife through the seasons.

Christchurch Park, situated just north of the centre of the mediaeval town of Ipswich, is used by many thousands of people for all sorts of recreation. The cultural heart of the Park is the Mansion, situated on the site of a former twelfth-century Augustinian monastery. This beautiful Elizabethan building now houses a hugely important collection of paintings and antiquities relating to the town of Ipswich. The Park's ponds and 82 acres of landscape are a continuing link with its history.

A vast number of events are arranged for everyone's enjoyment ranging from concerts for all tastes (including classical pop and folk music), dance and other cultural events. One of the highlights of the year is Music Day in July, and other celebrations include the Mela and the huge firework display organised by the Scouts in November. There is always something of interest going on. Apart from the formal events, the Park is a haven for people simply to enjoy themselves picnicking and relaxing. The children's play area is enormously popular and is an ideal place for grandparents to while away the time with their charges.

However, Christchurch Park is also hugely important for wildlife. In the centre of the Park the Wildlife Reserve, created over twenty years ago as the Bird Reserve, is being made ever more eco-friendly for its flora and fauna. The ponds, especially the Wilderness Pond, add considerably to the Park's enormously diverse wildlife.

The wellbeing of the natural history of Christchurch Park is very important and is constantly being monitored. We are blessed with a huge variety of wildlife here but, because of the activities in the Park over the course of the year and the sheer numbers of visitors to the area (45,000 on Music Day), the threat to wildlife is a constant worry. But so far, nature is coping. Of course some species fare better than others. At the moment I would say that it is the predators that are winning, for it seems that corvids (the crow family), large gulls and sparrowhawks, grey squirrels and foxes have adapted particularly well both to the environment and to the use of the Park by us humans. At the back of this book you will find a list of all the birds that have been seen here over the past fifty years. It includes some species that once found a home here but are now no longer present but also many more that we are still able to see, hear and enjoy.

Christchurch Park is unique and so is its wildlife, both of which are there for all to enjoy. But who knows what the future will bring?

Nuthatch

THE ORIGINS OF OUR BIRDS

British birds are made up of summer and winter visitors, passing migrants and those that reside here. We call our birds 'ours', but are they really? The summer birds are the ones that arrive here to breed in the spring. We regard as them as 'ours' because they build their nests, lay their eggs and rear their young here. But most summer visitors spend more time away from our shores than over here. Our swallows, for example, spend just as long, if not longer, below the equator in Africa and, for the people who live in those parts of Africa, the swallows are very much 'theirs'. Similarly, our winter visitors are not really ours. Although they spend the winter here, redwings and fieldfares are considered to be first and foremost birds of Scandinavia and Northern Europe. But does it really matter who lays claim to these birds?

So, where do our birds come from? Just like redwings and fieldfares, waxwings also come from Northern Europe and Scandinavia. But did you know that in the colder months the majority of our blackbirds also originate there? In winter, birds from the continent, particularly bullfinches, reinforce our finch population, and most over-wintering blackcaps have arrived the previous autumn from Germany.

If you look on the Round Pond in January, you will see lots of black-headed gulls (in winter plumage of course). These are not the resident birds you see in summer with chocolate brown heads. These winter birds bred in the Baltic, possibly Estonia, and have drifted down through the Baltic and North Sea in their thousands to winter in Britain – some of them in Christchurch Park. The Canada geese are resident, but originally they were North American birds, hence their name. They were kept over here in wildfowl collections and escapees have produced a British population. The Mandarin ducks likewise originally escaped from a collection, subsequently producing wild flocks of the species. The Mandarin is a wood duck and nests in holes in trees – that is why we have placed duck boxes in the trees on the islands of the Wilderness Pond. Our Mandarin duck population originates not from China but from a nearby wildfowl collection at the Victoria Nurseries in Westerfield Road!

We do have resident birds such as woodpeckers, magpies, crows, tawny owls, mallards and many more. But just pause when you see our summer or winter visitors and remember that many of them have travelled thousands of miles to be with us. Some are on their summer holidays, others have left the snows to be here. So, admire them, appreciate their beauty, but more than that admire their ability to travel those thousands of miles every year to give us pleasure. Finally, consider that those monster gulls that nest on the roof-tops in Ipswich and who upset people by 'scoffing' lots of the young mallards and moorhens in our Park are currently holidaying somewhere on the coast of West Africa.

Lesser black-backed gulls nesting in the chimney pots in High Street, Ipswich

THE PARK IS FOR EVERYONE

My notes are usually about wildlife and, in particular, birds. However, it was recently pointed out to me that quite a few of those who use Christchurch Park perhaps have little idea of which birds are around.

Birders can be a strange bunch of people; they are often dedicated to bird spotting and are generally extremely knowledgeable about their subject. Thus, it can be quite bewildering to these ornithologists that ordinary people can walk through the Park without recognising, say, a mistle thrush or even a magpie. Many people don't even see them – that feathered thing that flies across their vision or looks down at them from a hole in an oak tree remains, well, invisible.

So who uses Christchurch Park? Well, when the Park opens (or even when it is not) it is the dog walkers who first enjoy its beauty. The dogs are there for a reason, that is obvious, but they also exercise their owners as well. As stalwart Park man David Routh says, he meets the same owners and their dogs at the same time and place every day, rain or shine. To be one of the first people in the Park in the newness of morning is quite wonderful (as those who come to our annual Dawn Chorus Walk discover). Then there are those who traverse the Park on their way to work, having parked their cars in the surrounding roads, freeing their minds whilst walking through the Park.

There are also mums and children (with one or two dads of course) and, if parents are working, then there are grandparents helping out. Many of them head towards the play area, which is both good for the youngsters and a relief for their guardians. At the beginning of the soccer season, the flatter northern end of the Park is used by clubs for football training. It never ceases to amaze me how enthusiastic these sporty types are with goalposts made from well-positioned coats and no referees, training all out to prove their worthiness when playing in the Suffolk and Ipswich League. But don't listen too intently – football is a loud game nowadays and sometimes quite abusive. I've seen other sports being practised – cricket, rugby, athletics and Frisbee throwing, and what about the labours of the Boot Camp enthusiasts? And, yes, I nearly forgot the Father Christmas marathon runners.

These are just some of the Park users of the more casual variety. With the Fireworks' display, the ever-popular Music Day or the many other open-air events, then Christchurch Park is host to thousands of people. I dare say that few, if any, notice the calling nuthatches, preening stock doves or displaying moorhens. Encouragingly, despite all these visitors, wildlife still abounds. The Park is used to masses of people on occasions and tolerates the everyday visitor. When the footballers leave, flocks of redwing can be seen in late winter, foraging over the freshly raised stud-marked grass. Most people are unaware that just above their heads, birds are using holes in trees to breed or roost in, or that crows and magpies are scavenging among the shrubs and flowers. There are, however, just a few people who look for birds, listen to birds and, believe it or not, are oblivious to other human beings in the Park.

THE PARK'S MANDARIN DUCKS

The drake Mandarin is arguably the most beautiful of all ducks, although a case could be made for almost every duck. Our own (and very common) drake mallard is a very resplendent bird. My particular favourite is the shelduck, a bird that I associate with my childhood spent on the shores of the River Orwell at Nacton. The Mandarin is a wood duck, similar to the Carolina (an American wood duck) in that it nests in holes in trees, sometimes quite high from the ground. Its ducklings, being so light, come to no harm when they drop down to the ground below!

During the snowy weather of January 2010 when the country was in chaos, I walked past nearby Victoria Nurseries and on their very small pond were 14 Mandarin ducks waiting to be fed grain and pellets by Michael, the Nurseries' stockman. Now 14 ducks make for quite a large flock of Mandarins, but I do know that the Nurseries' flock includes those from our Park. Two questions now arise: what is the origin of these ducks, and if this flock at the Nurseries is larger than that of Christchurch Park, where do the others go?

Well, the first question can be answered quite easily. Michael says that when the pinioned Mandarin ducks were first introduced to the pond at Victoria Nurseries some 20 years ago, there was just one pair. A nest box was then put up and the pair successfully raised their young. Those young were also pinioned, or rather it was thought that they had been pinioned, but too late it was discovered that they could fly. The ducks discovered the Wilderness Pond and they would fly from the Nurseries back and forth to Christchurch Park, a distance of about half a mile. The Victoria Nurseries' pond was not only their birthplace but it was also there that they were regularly fed. That January, the maximum number of Mandarins I had seen on Christchurch Park was 9. Therefore up to 5 Mandarin ducks must have been resident somewhere else – Holywells Park perhaps? Incidentally, a fox killed the original pair. We know that breeding success has been achieved at Christchurch Park and, although not successfully reared, eggs have also been hatched at Holywells Park. It seems unlikely that a pair will now seek to raise young at the Nurseries.

The Mandarin is a beautiful duck and, to encourage more pairs to nest in Christchurch Park, 3 duck nesting boxes were placed on some of the trees on the islands of the Wilderness Pond. Strangely, whereas with mallard the males outnumber females by 4 or 5 to 1, the Mandarin ducks and drakes appear to be about equal in number. By February each year, they are already paired up with the males displaying and we can but hope for a good breeding season. Sadly, that success may depend on our friends, the lesser black-backed gulls.

During April and May 2010, up to 8 Mandarin ducks were seen on the Wilderness Pond with one pair always positioned near to the nesting Canada geese. During May, the female disappeared which suggested that she could have been incubating eggs. There seemed to be little promise of the other Mandarin ducks nesting as they were invariably sleeping or just preening. On 5 May, Mandarin ducks and a male Carolina duck, also a wood duck, appeared on the pond. The Mandarin ducks at first seemed to be a drake and two females but closer observation revealed that the two 'females' had the beginnings of orange sail feathers on their wings and black and white lines on their upper chests. Therefore, all three birds were males.

Ducks that hatch in the spring usually attain adult plumage after their first moult and they normally moult in

July/August when both male and female appear to be very similar. This is called the 'eclipse' period. In August 2009 there were 9 Mandarin ducks in moult on the Wilderness Pond. The two sub-adult males which appeared in May 2010 presented something of a mystery. Why were these birds not in adult plumage? Surely they were not young birds? If so, then they must have hatched in the middle of our very severe winter. Surely not! An explanation for this may be found in Peter Scott's *Key to the Wildfowl of the World* in which he says, "Male wood duck can spend several months in dull plumage usually resembling the female. Intermediate plumage occurs during this transition." So, whereas most duck attain summer plumage after the summer moult, it appears that some wood duck take much longer. This answers the question of why in the breeding season some drake Mandarin ducks resemble females and are not in their usually resplendent attire.

On 26 May 2010, freshly-hatched Mandarin ducklings appeared on the south side of the Wilderness Pond with a female and one of the dull-plumaged males in attendance. The female was very agitated, calling softly, occasionally coming out of the water and padding through the undergrowth at the water's edge. An adult male, in full plumage, was very close by but seemed completely disinterested. It was obvious that the female had paired up with a sub-adult male. A female mallard nearby had a brood of ducklings that I am sure contained at least three Mandarin ducklings. The adult and young Mandarins came ashore and stood no more than a metre away from me. On 11 June, the two young Mandarins were 16 days old. Their survival had been down to the dedication of their parents. It seems that the female Mandarin took charge of one duckling, the sub-adult male the other. Mandarins can be extremely aggressive towards other waterfowl. The vast majority of Canada goslings were eaten by herring and lesser black-backed gulls. All of the young mallard also disappeared but when the large gulls tried to get to the Mandarin ducklings the spare drake Mandarins on the Wilderness Pond joined in their defence. Later, the large gulls predated all of the mallard brood, including the three commandeered wood duck.

As summer 2010 progressed, so the number of Mandarin ducks on the two ponds increased. At the beginning of July, some of the Mandarin ducks had begun their annual moult and 11 ducks were on the Wilderness Pond. By the end of July all the Mandarin ducks were in moult, and it was very difficult to tell the difference between males and females. On 6 August, 12 Mandarins were counted on the Wilderness Pond islands and by the 8 August there were 17. By the 10 August the total numbers increased to 27 with the arrival of 10 immature ducks on the Round Pond. This I believe to be a Suffolk record. On 25 August, there were 12 immature Mandarin ducks on the Round Pond which I thought could be the young from a pair in Holywells Park. A quite phenomenal breeding success and now another mystery was solved. I believe the build-up of ducks in our Park may be because the Mandarin ducks in the Ipswich area come here to moult. The Wilderness Pond is a large area of open water, relatively safe from predators. Perhaps the immature birds arrived en masse from Holywells Park with adult birds since, by the end of August although they had not completed their moult, most ducks were able to fly. By 10 September, the Mandarins ducks began to disperse with just 12 remaining.

The Carolina duck also disappeared after its moult, but a female tufted duck turned up. Now, tufted duck bred on the Holywells Ponds that year, so perhaps it took wing and came to Christchurch Park with the Mandarin ducks. I know for a fact that serious birdwatchers come to Christchurch Park just to observe the Mandarin ducks. Although wild birds, they are very obliging and will readily pose for photographs.

WOOD DUCK OF CHRISTCHURCH PARK.

TWO SPECIES OF WOOD DUCK VISIT OUR PARK - ONE, THE MANDARIN IS NOW OFFICIALLY A BRITISH WILD BIRD - THE OTHER, THE CAROLINA IS RECOGNISED AS AN ESCAPEE.

WOOD DUCK NEST IN HOLES IN TREES - OR DUCK BOXES.

MALE CAROLINA
A SINGLE MALE VISITS THE PARK

FEMALE MANDARIN

MANDARIN
ORIGINALLY FROM CHINA - PERHAPS THE MOST BEAUTIFUL OF ALL DUCKS - BREEDS IN OUR PARK

MANDARIN CAN OFTEN BE SEEN PERCHED ON THE POSTS OF THE WILDERNESS POND ISLANDS. THESE DUCKS REACH A PEAK IN MID-SUMMER WHEN UP TO 27 CAN BE SEEN DURING THEIR MOULT.

REG SNOOK 2010.

WORKING IN THE PARK IN WINTER

During one particularly cold winter spell, three gallant FoCP volunteers, together with Park Ranger Laura Whitfield, carried out some sterling work in the Wildlife Reserve. Thirty-five bird boxes were put up in the trees to replace boxes which, over 20 years, had deteriorated. We then visited the islands in the Wilderness Pond taking down most of the wire-netting fencing that had prevented the ducks and geese from nesting. Some netting remained – a job for another winter. Finally, we put up 4 duck boxes on trees on the islands to encourage the Mandarin ducks to nest.

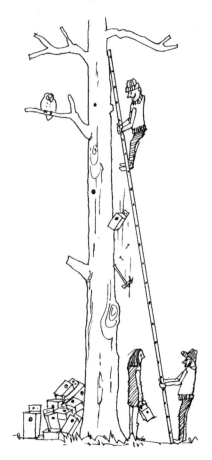

One interesting 'find' whilst doing this work was a dead black-headed gull which carried a ring on one of its legs. This indicated that the gull had been ringed in Stockholm, Sweden on 17 April 2007. The British Trust for Ornithology subsequently informed us that, when ringed, this bird was of unknown sex and aged between 2 and 3 years. The distance between Stockholm and Christchurch Park is 870 km.

When we did this work we discovered that some of the old nest boxes had been reinforced with metal plates to prevent great spotted woodpeckers from enlarging the holes in order to destroy the contents. Despite this, however, continual hammering by the woodpeckers had produced deep gouges in the metal and the holes had still been enlarged.

In early February 2010, butterfly expert Richard Stewart (who lives close to the Park) saw two blackcaps in his garden, one male and one female. I mention this because only a few years ago this would have been a very rare occurrence at this time of the year in these parts. However, the sighting of blackcaps in winter is now fairly common. This is because many of the blackcaps in continental Europe, particularly Germany, now migrate west and not south in winter, with many ending up in Britain. Although the blackcap is a warbler, and therefore an insect eater, it is seen more and more on garden bird feeders eating peanuts. Some call the blackcap the 'northern nightingale' because of its delightful song, and the bird often features in the Friends of Christchurch Park Dawn Chorus walks that are held annually around the beginning of May.

But as early as 4 March 2010, Philip Murphy (who compiled the detailed bird list at the back of this book) saw a male blackcap in nearby Tuddenham Road and it was singing its heart out! Roll on spring!

MABEL

Mabel is a large female tawny owl. She was first seen in 2008, perched at the entrance of a hole in an old oak tree, on full view to all. She always seemed to be there, and was named Mabel as a result of a competition. Thousands saw her and she was much photographed – in fact she became a national treasure when her picture appeared in the Daily Mail. In 2009, Mabel produced offspring and she became probably the most loved bird in the Ipswich area.

March 2010: it looks as though we may have lost Mabel. In early February her roosting place was empty. As the days went by it became evident that something serious might have happened to our favourite tawny owl. On February 10, a grey squirrel was seen sitting in the space that Mabel had occupied for the previous 18 months. So what has happened to her? It could be that Mabel has chosen a new roosting place or that she is incubating eggs, although it seems a bit early for that. Of course, she might have met with an accident. Tawny owls are predators and sometimes they come to grief whilst out hunting. Being a town owl, her food probably consists mainly of rodents and therefore it is conceivable that she could have been poisoned. There is another possibility. With the prolonged cold spell she could have found it impossible to find food and unfortunately starved to death. I am only surmising what could have happened. My own opinion is that her food supply might have run out in the bad weather and she has found a better source of food and is roosting in a new area. These are just a few of the possibilities – perhaps we will never know.

Mabel was, and still remains, a star!

*Mabel – our special
tawny owl*

May 2010: the good news for local tawny owl fans is that our nationally-known heroine, Mabel, may still be resident in Christchurch Park!

On 20 May, Park Manager Sam Pollard was informed by a visitor to the Park that a baby tawny owl was clinging to the trunk of an ancient chestnut tree very close to the Reg Driver Visitor Centre. You can only imagine Sam's surprise and delight when he saw, four feet up in the tree, a young tawny owl. Sam quickly photographed the young bird and the owl was subsequently placed higher in the tree for its own safety.

Coincidentally, at exactly the same time in 2009 a baby tawny owl had been found at the foot of the tree of Mabel's roost. It seems highly likely that this new baby owl might be Mabel's offspring, who herself may now be resident in a different tree somewhere near to her previous home. One cannot be certain of this, but I want to think that Mabel is alive and well! However, the excellent news is that, whatever the truth, we still have tawny owls nesting in our Park.

November 2010: in October, reports came in that a tawny owl had been seen in Mabel's old roost. At first, the owl's appearances were intermittent but soon she was being seen more often. But was this Mabel? In early November, local photographer Catherine Howard-Dobson took a picture of the tawny owl and compared it with one she had taken almost exactly two years previously. In my opinion, the two owls looked identical – so Mabel had not gone away.

August 2011: after another few months when we all feared for Mabel's well-being, she is back. Once again, passers-by are able to look up and say "Good Morning" to a truly amazing bird.

WOODPECKERS, WOODIES AND WATERHENS

The great spotted woodpecker is the black and white one that lives in the wooded area of Christchurch Park. It is about the size of a blackbird, has red under its tail and the rest of the plumage is black and white (the male also has a red patch on his nape). This woodpecker is renowned for its 'drumming' which is first heard towards the end of December and that reaches its peak in the spring. Our only other woodpecker is the green woodpecker, a bird about the size of a jackdaw, which is found more often than not on the open grassy areas of the Park feeding on ants. This bird has green upper parts and yellow under parts with a red crown, black eye-stripe and moustache. Its flight is undulating, its voice unmistakable – a long, drawn-out series of laughs – hence its country name of 'yaffle'. Sadly, the lesser spotted woodpecker has declined so badly in recent years that it can no longer be found in our Park.

Do you love pigeons or do you hate them? The wood pigeon is a beautiful bird but it is not everybody's favourite. Farmers really hate them! There is no doubt that wood pigeons eat lots of young kale and ripe corn – but I say "so what!" Local wood pigeon numbers are increased in the winter months by the millions that come over from the continent. Shooters and bird scarers seem to have little effect on the damage done by 'woodies'. Wood pigeons are common in the Park – they are the fat, grey birds that seem to prefer to waddle over the grass rather than fly. They are loved and they are not loved! But imagine if you will, a hot summer's day – not a cloud in the sky – having a picnic in the Park and being serenaded by a big, fat, cooing pigeon. Now that pigeon is really a dove, sometimes called a ring dove because of the white flashes on its neck. A close relative is the stock dove, also found in our Park. This bird has no white bars on its neck and, unlike its cousin, it nests in holes in trees. The other pigeon (or rather dove) is the collared dove; smaller than the other two. It is brown and grey with a black band on its neck. Now, if you go into the centre of Ipswich you will find feral pigeons, the 'liquorice allsorts' of the pigeon world. These are racing or homing pigeons which have become wild and they are a feature of most cities and towns. A mixture of blue, red, black and white, these birds are a serious nuisance owing to their droppings on buildings in Ipswich.

The moorhen is sometimes known as the waterhen and is the small water bird found on or near our Wilderness and Round Ponds. This dark plumaged bird has a bright red and yellow beak and ridiculously long feet. It usually nests in vegetation near water but can nest in some strange places – like the drain that leaks into the Round Pond or in the flotsam that collects by the water's edge of the Wilderness Pond. I have found moorhen nests high up in trees (one was even in an old crow's nest). When I was a boy, my father would encourage me to search for moorhen nests – he liked half a dozen moorhen's eggs for breakfast with his bacon! (You must remember that this was post-war austerity when chicken eggs were hard to come by.) An interesting and unique situation that occurs when a moorhen has a second brood of youngsters is that the young from the first brood will help their parents raise their newly-hatched siblings.

Stock dove, collared dove and wood pigeon

BIRDSONG AND 'SPARS'

At a recent AGM of the Friends of Christchurch Park, Malcolm Clark gave an extremely interesting talk on the birdsong of the Park. Malcolm has been recording birdsong for many years. It is comforting to know that there is someone else recording the birds of the Park but coming at it from a slightly different angle. Recording birdsong is not just a case of sticking a microphone in the air and hoping that a bird will come near enough for a few 'tweets' to be recorded. On the contrary, first and foremost the recorder has to be a competent ornithologist, and Malcolm is just such a man. His knowledge of the birds of this area is first-class and, unlike many birdwatchers, he also knows his birdsong. Both he and Philip Murphy regularly visit our Park just to listen!

At his talk, Malcolm included recordings of three of the Park's 'specialist birds', one of which was the nuthatch. This bird has a wide range of call notes, and Malcolm managed to record them all. In the Park, nuthatches can be found in the oak trees near to the Westerfield Road entrance. Malcolm suggested that they look rather like a poor man's kingfisher because of their colouring. Unusually, they also climb down trees. Another bird Malcolm recorded was the Mandarin duck – a beautiful duck that can be quite vocal. Finally, Malcolm played us recordings made in the previous year in the Wildlife Reserve of sparrowhawks which had nested in the large fir trees and raised three young.

Now, the sparrowhawk! This bird is causing a good deal of controversy as sparrowhawks eat smaller birds. The RSPB and other ornithological societies have been inundated with protests from people suggesting that 'spars' are responsible for the decline of our songbirds. Songbirds are definitely in decline but are sparrowhawks really to blame? The RSPB says that sparrowhawks alone are not culpable for the loss of yellowhammer, bullfinch, lesser spotted woodpecker, house sparrow and a host of other songbirds. Other reasons for their decline include loss of habitat, changing farming methods, and less scrub areas. But to return to Christchurch Park and our pair of spars with their three fledged youngsters: how many songbirds must be taken per day to feed these five birds of prey? Multiply that number by each day of the year and you do have a lot of dead songbirds. If songbird numbers are at an all time low and sparrowhawks are flourishing, then no wonder some people feel that bird societies may not be seeing the whole picture.

For the past 29 years I have been a Wildlife Inspector for the Department of the Environment, which became DEFRA and then Animal Health as it is now known. Specialising in birds of prey, I love them! But I am looking at the problem from the eyes of those who have seen the majority of their garden birds disappear, and just maybe this is due to sparrowhawks.

The Sparrowhawk – the enemy of our songbirds?

MY HOME IS A HOLE IN A TREE

Recently, the Friends helped to put up 35 bird boxes in the Wildlife Reserve with a view to ensuring that there were enough nesting sites for birds during the forthcoming breeding seasons. One of the main features of Christchurch Park is the large amount of really old trees that are full of various holes, nooks and crannies, vital to many of the Park's avian residents. I'm certain that without these the bird population of our Park would be very different from what we have today.

I thought I would mention a few of our hole-nesting birds, some very obvious and others not so. Perhaps the most obvious, because of a certain winged celebrity, is the tawny owl. Despite Mabel's occasional disappearance from the scene, I believe that we have at least two pairs in or nearby the Park. Judging by the calls heard during the evening and night, I would not be at all surprised if this was a conservative estimate bearing in mind that the Park area includes the old cemetery and the wooded gardens of houses to the north. Another obvious hole-nesting bird is the jackdaw whose numbers are on the increase, probably because of ample food and plenty of nesting places. Many large older houses have unused chimneys nowadays and jackdaws will readily fill these up with twigs to form a nesting platform. So, if there are insufficient holes in the trees of Christchurch Park for them, then the jackdaws will use these disused chimney pots. The jackdaw is a member of the crow family and is the only crow in this area that nests in a hole, as we have neither choughs nor ravens here.

The only member of the dove (or pigeon) family that readily nests in holes in trees is the stock dove. This is the delightful little bluey/grey dove with no white neck flashes but instead, a beautiful green and mauve sheen on its neck. Smaller than its more obvious cousin the wood pigeon, the stock dove is increasing in numbers and has already colonised at least one of our duck boxes! Blue and great tits don't only nest in man-made boxes: careful observation in late spring will see both of these species breeding in cavities all over the Park. The coal tit, a bird usually associated with the Park's fir trees, is also a hole-nesting bird, but not as common as these other two titmice. The coal tit is worth looking at because, although at first glance it seems a brown and black plumaged bird, it has in fact a plumage of delicate shades of pastel browns and pink.

One of the Park's most famous hole-nesting species is the nuthatch. What is so special about this wonderful little bird, besides its extremely smart blue and orange appearance, is its nesting habit. Once a hole has been located in which the eggs are to be laid, the nuthatch then uses mud to make the hole small enough to allow only itself to enter and not the majority of its predators (e.g. squirrel). The robin, Britain's favourite bird, will nest in a tree hole, an old kettle, a watering can, an old Wellington boot or even in a nest box. The wren, that small brown bird with a very loud voice, will readily nest in a small hole in a tree or, for that matter, a bird box. Unfortunately, we have now lost one of my favourite Park birds – the friendly spotted flycatcher. This bird does not nest in holes, but if a hole is shallow enough it will make use of it as a nesting ledge. The FoCP have positioned six treecreeper nesting boxes in the Wildlife Reserve. This small brown bird, which has a curved beak, usually builds a nest where the bark of a tree has come away from the trunk. However, it will also use a bird box. The observer might think that a box shaped like a wedge of cheese and hammered to a tree trunk about 10 feet from the ground has no chance of enticing a bird to nest in it. We shall see!

Over the last decade, numbers of starling and house sparrow have slumped. Both will nest in holes in trees, and a few appear to be centred on the old sweet chestnuts near to the Reg Driver Centre. Two other iconic hole-nesting birds are the great spotted and green woodpeckers. They hollow out holes in tree boughs in which to lay their eggs. Strangely enough, one of my larger nest boxes was used by a green woodpecker in which to rear its young.

Finally, when we were working on the Wilderness Pond islands one February, we saw a female mallard with a clutch of eggs in a hollow willow tree. When you are casually walking through the Park on a warm spring day, keep an eye out for holes in trees and see what pops out!

STAG BEETLES AND BILLY-WITCHES

On balmy June evenings many, many years ago, our gang (mainly consisting of 7 to 9 year olds) would gather up our old tennis rackets and head for an ungainly wild plum hedge. Our goal? To knock down as many 'billy-witches' as we could! These flying beetles, real name cockchafers, would fly amongst the branches in their thousands. Only we brave boys would go hunting for billy-witches because they were thought to trap themselves in the hair of small girls! The thing about these flying beetles is that their legs and feet have very small hooks which give them the ability to cling very tightly to clothes, and it is not at all easy to pull them off. So, we would fill jam jars full of these crawling beetles and then, being horrible little boys, we would empty them over the heads of small girls!

Occasionally while we were hunting cockchafers we would see stag beetles. These magnificent creatures were far more common in those days and we never attempted to smash them with our tennis rackets. In fact, 7 year-old boys were quite scared of stag beetles and we never even collected them. However, we did love to watch them in the air since they are very slow flyers. They do not move horizontally but travel with their abdomen much lower than their head, almost as though they really find it difficult to stay airborne. They must be slow flyers because I can easily overtake a stag beetle on my bike, and I am no Lance Armstrong!

Stag beetles are magnificent creatures, coloured brown and black with a purple tinge. They are Britain's largest beetle. The antlers give them their name although, despite the size of their antlers, the males are harmless. The females of the species do not have such large antlers but, surprisingly, they are capable of giving a nasty nip. Their eggs are laid in rotten wood, usually oak. The larvae spend three years there before turning into pupae and it is another year before the adult emerges. It used to be thought that adult stag beetles buried themselves into the ground for the winter before emerging again in the spring. Sadly, an adult stag beetle's life is limited to a few months at best. We have stag beetles in our Park, though not as many as there were in the past. However, in the Wildlife Reserve, the Park Rangers have provided piles of rotting wood to encourage stag beetles to lay their eggs in the decaying timber.

There is another stag beetle – the lesser stag beetle. This beetle is black, and both sexes are similar. Its life cycle is like that of its larger cousin but the lesser stag beetle is far more common in this area. It is usually seen on the ground and not in the air.

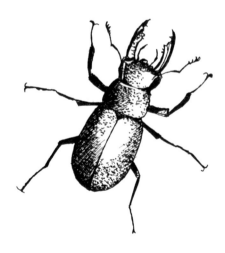

The stag beetle

SUMMER IS COMING!

The cold wind drops, the sun comes out, it is warmer and the football season nears its end. However, men in varying plumage (mostly blue and white) are still kicking footballs about, using jackets as goalposts – so traditional! Perhaps it's because of the IPL series in India that cricket has reappeared too – 20-20 is all the rage now. This is Christchurch Park, soon to be host to the likes of Jools Holland and Kathryn Jenkins, later the FoCP summer band concerts in the Upper Arboretum and many other events. Summer is coming. Is it not wonderful that our Park can be used for so many events and by so many people?

So how does nature cope with all this activity? Quite well really. It comes as no surprise to birds and animals that live in the Park to find both fit and unfit young men choosing to belt a plastic or leather ball about on the grassy slopes; only occasionally a misplaced clearance will dislodge a sleeping pigeon or scatter a family party of starlings. So long as the more wild areas are respected, then everything is fine.

Sadly, when work was carried out one winter on the Wilderness Pond islands, all sorts of rubbish was found – bottles, cans, mobile phones and even a wallet (empty). When the water was iced over at New Year, all manner of objects were used to try and break the ice including a Park bench! One of the worst types of rubbish is the plastic bag, which is dangerous to wildlife and highly visible to the public eye. In the past, drug-related items have been found in certain areas of the Wildlife Reserve but thanks to police surveillance and a regular patrol by Park security officers this problem has been greatly reduced. It seems also that the problem of graffiti is not too bad – I hope I haven't spoken too soon...

On a much more pleasant note, one sunny day in mid-April I sat on a log beside the Wilderness Pond and quietly watched the smaller park birds. Very active was a goldcrest searching through pine needles, whilst loudly calling was a great tit followed by a blackcap. A wren burst into song and then I saw a treecreeper in the tree next to me. All this time a chiffchaff was monotonously repeating its name. Robin, dunnock and blue tit made the total nine, and double figures were reached when a long-tailed tit arrived to collect lichen for its nest. Ten resplendent smaller birds, all of which had been seen just by sitting on a log by the pond. Of course, the background noise was still of quacking mallard, honking geese and mewing gulls but you can't have everything.

It seems that kestrels have decided against trying to nest in our Park this year and although I've heard tawny owls calling, it is not going to be as easy as last year to confirm breeding. It also looks as though our efforts to encourage Mandarins to breed are a failure this time – perhaps due to grey squirrels. Hopefully, Mandarins will come back to the Wilderness Pond to moult. However, careful observations may prove me wrong – we shall see.

A goldcrest – the Park's smallest bird

Nesting long-tailed tits

THESE BIRDS HAVE FLOWN...

For the last two years there have been no spotted flycatchers in Christchurch Park. Quite a simple statement really, but they were one of the Park's most interesting nesting birds. Friendly creatures, beautiful little summer visitors that came here from Africa to raise a family, but now they have gone. So what, you might ask? Does it really matter?

Well, let me try and answer that question by explaining the situation of yet another once common bird. When I was a boy (not so long ago really, I like to think) the red-backed shrike was also a common and handsome summer visitor. Most young boys collected birds' eggs at that time and everyone I knew had a shrike's egg. The main reason was that the red-backed shrike built its nest in such an easily accessible position. It was a bird that frequented allotments, gardens and hedgerows consisting of mature hawthorn bushes. The male shrike would give its position away by perching on top of the bush or small tree, and its colouring made it obvious to the observer. The nest was similar in shape to that of a blackbird but usually more bulky, and I once found one that was made almost entirely of shredded paper that had previously been used as packing. I suppose the shrike chose hawthorn in which to build its nest because of the thorns which offered the bird some sort of protection. However, those thorns also offered the shrike the opportunity to build itself a larder by piercing bumblebees and lizards on the spikes. The red-backed shrike was common then but gradually it became less so. Now it no longer nests in Suffolk or indeed in the rest of England.

The spotted flycatcher was similar in status to the red-backed shrike (maybe even more common), but sadly it seems to be disappearing in the same way. Last year, I found only one spotted flycatcher's nest. It has gone from being a bird that regularly nested in roadside ivy-clad trees, in gardens, on ledges over backdoors, in porches, in rose bushes that clung to walls and even on top of bird boxes, to being a bird that is rapidly disappearing. Our Park is a typical habitat that always had its spotted flycatchers – a habitat that in theory appears ideal with mature oak trees, grassy areas and a seemingly plentiful supply of insect food. But, nevertheless, they have gone.

Does it matter? Why should we worry about a little brown bird that no longer comes to Christchurch Park? Well, the red-backed shrike has disappeared, the spotted flycatcher has now gone and so has the lesser spotted woodpecker. The hawfinch, tree sparrow and the turtle dove are no more, and so the list goes on. Birds which were once very common are fast disappearing. Some will say that the loss of a few species of birds does not affect the way we live, and makes no difference to us at all. Many wouldn't recognise a spotted flycatcher even if it jumped up and bit one on the nose. So why bother or get upset at its loss? There are still plenty of birds to be seen – pigeons, crows, magpies, geese and ducks.

When the reign of our tawny owl Mabel appeared to have come to an end, people were genuinely upset. They would look up to where Mabel once sat and feel sad that she had disappeared from their lives. To a few of us 'birdy' people, the loss of a little brown bird has the same effect.

The hawfinch – one of the birds
that used to visit our Park

NOTHING SHOULD SURPRISE US

A few days ago, I caught the end of the programme *The Weakest Link*, when Anne Robinson posed the question to one of the finalists: "What large waterfowl is named after the naturalist Thomas Bewick?" Back came the reply: "Dunnock". Now, a dunnock is a small brown hedgerow bird and a Bewick's swan is a very large waterfowl. Ah, well..!

I recently met some friends by the Wilderness Pond who were watching the wildfowl feeding. I casually asked them if they knew what species they were looking at. I was amazed at their replies. They knew that the large birds were geese of some kind, but not that they were Canada geese; they recognised the mallard as ducks but not what kind of fowl, and, astonishingly to me, they had no idea what moorhens looked like. Now, I do realise that I am a 'birdie type' – though I like to think I am not of the 'anorak' fraternity – but I thought that most people had a rough idea of what common birds could be seen locally. I therefore decided to conduct my own mini poll of people using the Park just to see what my friends knew. To me, the results were remarkable! It made me realise that most people are completely oblivious of the bird-life of the Park. Although a few were quite knowledgeable, most were not. One person knew about kingfishers and herons but thought that a kingfisher was the same size as a heron. One person thought that all of our mallard may have escaped from captivity; another had no idea that the crow family consisted of several species or that robins inhabited the Park.

With all the coverage that wildlife gets on television I had expected that most people would have a good idea of local birdlife. Both *Springwatch* and *Autumnwatch* are viewed avidly by millions of people and parts of the programmes are often locally based – that is if you consider Norfolk to be local. Over the years, David Attenborough has lifted the profile of nature programmes and, with the RSPB and Suffolk Wildlife Trust promoting all sorts of local events, I would have thought that most people might have had a good knowledge of natural history. It emphasises to me that when I was a young boy, large periods of school time were devoted entirely to nature, and that included birdwatching. Yes, we did collect birds' eggs, but birds were far more common then. Even egg collecting increased our knowledge, and although of course I am strongly against that activity these days, I am of the opinion that sitting in front of the 'box' is no substitute for actually watching wildlife.

As a keen birdman, it saddens me to find that people enjoying our wonderful Park and its facilities seem unaware of just what is singing or flying around them. However, they could likewise be justified in criticising me for my ignorance of modern technology, and might well consider me as being stuck in the past. But not recognising a robin or a Canada goose does surprise me. Several people that I spoke with did identify the overhead white birds as being gulls – well seagulls actually – but there are many species of gull, four of which may be seen in Christchurch Park, and they can hardly be called seagulls. When it came to mammals, most thought that grey squirrels were wonderful and they loved foxes, but several considered bats to be repulsive and scary. Once again, I feel that previous methods of education may have helped to allay people's fear of bats. But saddest of all was that not one person could name three trees correctly – oak and ash became muddled and some thought that many of the Park's trees were elm. It is obvious that times have changed far more than one realises from my youth, when I had the freedom to roam the countryside without fear.

BIRD LIFE IN THE PARK

Y ou don't have to wear the birdwatchers' 'uniform' to see interesting bird behaviour in the Park. There is no need for anorak, woolly hat and binoculars! The other day I bought an ice-cream from the Pavilion near Westerfield Road and sat on one of the nearby benches to eat it. At first glance, there appeared to be very little bird activity whatsoever apart from a couple of fat wood pigeons trundling over the grass and a family of excited magpies looking for insects. Three lesser black-backed gulls were also on the grass just standing there, apparently not interested in anything in particular. Suddenly, flying low across the area and at some speed, there was a brown flash – a sparrowhawk? No! A mistle thrush no less. This large thrush flew straight at the gulls and appeared to strike one of them on its back. The gulls, obviously very surprised, took off and flew away towards the ponds. A mistle thrush attacking three large gulls? Why? Did the thrush consider the gulls to be a threat? Were they recognised as predators? Well, it was certainly a change for these gulls to be on the receiving end of such behaviour.

However, the mistle thrush did not escape entirely without a little bit of aggro itself. After its assault on the gulls, the thrush began searching for food on the grass in front of the Pavilion. Amazingly, it received some of its own treatment when a male chaffinch began dive-bombing in a quite ferocious and relentless attack. The mistle thrush decided that it had had enough for one day and beat a hasty retreat.

June and July are good months to see family parties of adult birds with their young. Last summer, a pair of goldfinches had built their beautiful little nest in the top of a mountain ash tree, again near the ice-cream Pavilion. The fledged young were with their parents searching for seed-heads. By this time of year, adult birds can begin to look somewhat ragged due to the rigours of rearing young, but that summer the adult goldfinches still outshone their youngsters who had not yet attained the black and red head-dress. Despite recent severe winters, our smaller song bird numbers are holding up, and wrens, long-tailed tits, goldcrests and other tit family members have had good breeding seasons of late.

Many people have remarked recently on the large number of singing blackcaps. I know that many nests have been found in gardens surrounding our Park, and chiffchaffs can always be heard singing in the Wildlife Reserve. Another summer visitor which has arrived in large numbers is a warbler – the common whitethroat. Birdwatchers had been concerned about its falling numbers but last year there was a huge increase. The hedgerows and roadside verges in Suffolk are alive with its scratchy song. I don't know the reason for this sudden build-up but it is very welcome. Sadly, our Park does not provide the right habitat for the whitethroat to nest but, well, you never know with birds.

Mistle thrush

SUMMER IN THE PARK WITH TREECREEPERS

On the day before one July Music Day (when annually upwards of 45,000 people come to the Park), I walked through the tents, marquees, lorries and stage sets to the edge of the Wildlife Reserve. Loudspeakers and miles of rubber-coated leads hung from the trees and pseudo performers were testing the sound systems, filling the air with out-of-tune noise and off-key lyrics. Yet, above all this mayhem, I heard several thin, high-pitched calls and I knew that I had come across a family of treecreepers.

Although treecreepers are secretive, small brown birds, it is not unusual to see them in our Park, especially during June and July. They stay together in close-knit parties and often the young from the first clutch will hang around with the young from the second. You can often discover twelve or so birds in one party, and what makes them easy to find is that they call to each other all the time as they hunt for food. The family that I saw numbered a dozen and they were flitting through the Scots pines and horse chestnuts like large brown moths. We feared for these delightful birds during the recent harsh winters, thinking they would not survive the prolonged cold weather. But survive they did, and with good breeding success. It is difficult to say just how many pairs of treecreepers we have in the Park but on that day I saw two family flocks numbering at least twenty birds, and there are probably many more than that in Christchurch Park.

The treecreeper is well adapted for life in a wood or forest. Its plumage is mainly brown, spotted with both lighter and darker marks, which makes it hard to be seen on the bark of a tree. However, it is always on the move, searching the bark for insects that it digs out of the crevices with a thin, down-curved beak. Another identification characteristic of this little bird is that it flies to the lower part of the tree-trunk and then climbs up jerkily in a spiral motion. When in a flock with others it calls continuously. It has been described at times as being mouse like but I do not think that this is an accurate description. On the trunk of a tree it looks, well, like a bird and in flight it cannot be mistaken for a bat. One other feature is its tail, which has stiff central feathers, very much like that of a woodpecker, which it uses for support when climbing.

During one winter, FoCP members with Park Ranger Laura, placed six nest boxes, shaped like wedges of cheese, in the Reserve. Designed especially to attract treecreepers, it is hoped that they will find these boxes very like their natural nesting habitat. They usually nest behind bark that has come away slightly from the trunk, affording the sitting female and young protection from beady-eyed predators. The young all leave the nest together and will then roost together, tightly packing themselves in a depression in the bark.

It seems that our treecreepers are doing very well. If you have not acquainted yourself with them, then it is well worth a search. Be quiet, look and listen and you will surely see these wonderful little birds either climbing up the trunks of trees or flitting through the dappled light of the Wildlife Reserve, calling as they go. Small brown birds they may be but they are also one of Christchurch Park's stars. Strangely, I have little information on the recent wellbeing of our nuthatches for which our Park is well known. Last spring, they were very vociferous but it appears that this last breeding season of nuthatches has not been as successful as that of the treecreepers. I hope I am wrong.

WE ARE NOT AS CLEVER AS WE THINK

I sometimes have my doubts over people who are referred to as 'experts'. Rather embarrassingly, I am occasionally described as an expert on birds, or an expert naturalist. Now the trouble here is that we can never know it all, as nature does not always conform and, quite often, the 'norm' inexplicably becomes the 'abnormal'. I should never say that a bird will do such and such a thing; the chances are that it will conform, but to say that it will do something simply opens the door for it to do something completely alien to its lifestyle. A good example of this was when I was told of a kingfisher eating grapes! No, that simply does not happen. But it did, and others have now also recorded kingfishers doing the same thing: one instance took place in a greenhouse in Berners Street, Ipswich. In the early days of the Suffolk Ornithologists' Group, one observer saw a little owl actually following a plough looking for worms. Another time, several of us went to the Brecks in Norfolk, where we saw a long-eared owl hunting in the middle of the day in bright sunlight. As most ornithologists know, the long-eared owl is supposed to be a true night owl.

Ornithology is littered with birds doing things that they should simply not be doing. Quickly the 'expert' learns that to be adamant about a bird never doing something means that he will soon be proved wrong. The same applies to bird sightings. If someone reports a sighting of, say, a cuckoo in December, then although that sighting may be extremely unlikely, there is just a chance that it may be correct. Many years ago, I received reports of gannets flying over the fields just east of Ipswich. I told the observer that he had probably just seen large gulls. A few days later, he brought to me a gannet which had struck overhead wires hung between the pylons to the north-east of Ipswich. I had got it wrong again.

*A kingfisher – one of Christchurch
Park's most handsome visitors*

So, the naturalist can often be made a fool of. I mention this because at the end of June I was doing my usual tour of the Wilderness Pond. I was checking the Mandarins when I saw a Dad and his 5 year-old daughter by the small rock gardens just below the Bowling Green where there is a dribbling waterfall. The daughter was standing by the little wooden bridge ankle deep in the water, whilst her father was overlooking the situation holding a net. I asked the young girl what she was looking for. "Frogs", the young girl replied. "There are no frogs here", I said. Well, perhaps I should have bitten my tongue because the youngster then held up a jar containing some young frogs and a newt. I had no idea that frogs and newts lived there. So much for being a nature 'know-all'!

Swifts fascinate me and I eagerly await their return to breed here. They usually arrive back in the second week of May and then they quickly get down to rearing young. In June and July I see screaming swifts as they zoom between the chimney pots of my neighbours' houses. Now, all of you, look skywards. Look up and see these 'devil' birds scything through the sky catching insects. Hurry up – by mid-August they will be gone.

In July of most years we are in the middle of the moulting season for our ducks, called the 'eclipse' period. This is when the ducks shed their old feathers and gain new ones. Look at the ducks on the Wilderness Pond and you will see that the male mallard is a dowdy brown colour, making it almost indistinguishable from the female. However, the male mallard has a yellowish bill and, at that time of the year, this is almost the only way in which to recognise the drake. In September, the males will regain their splendid colouring.

WOODIES

Woodpeckers make me smile, I don't really know why, I just think that they are rather amusing, even comical. I love the way that they can cling to the bark of a tree and jerkily climb upwards, occasionally pausing to glance at the observer. Luckily, it seems that both of our woodpeckers, green and great spotted, have had good breeding seasons recently. Adults and young can be seen in Christchurch Park, and heard too, for both species can be fairly noisy.

The green woodpecker is the larger of the two. This is the one that 'laughs' or 'yaffles'. At a pop concert in the Park in late July one year, just as Rick Astley was belting out his huge hit "Never gonna give you up", a green woodpecker flew over the Park laughing. Whether or not it was laughing at Rick or was just enjoying the music I will never know, but I bet it did not hang around when the fireworks started. (Why do fireworks have to be so loud? Why can't they just be pretty?) The green woodpecker is easily recognised because it is, well, green and it is the woodpecker that you see on the grassy areas towards the north of our Park. It seldom drums, instead it laughs. It is a beautiful woodpecker with a green back and wings, bright yellow rump and a red head with a black moustache. The under parts are pale yellow. Only one brood is produced, with usually five to seven eggs in a clutch. Of course, the eggs are laid in a hole in either a trunk or a branch of a tree. Surprisingly, I have succeeded in getting green woodpeckers to make their home in a bird box. When these birds are seen on the ground, they can sometimes be confused with mistle thrushes as both birds hold themselves upright. In flight, however, the bird is unmistakable. It moves with an exaggerated, undulating flight and appears to be very heavy.

A green woodpecker making its mark

The great spotted woodpecker is smaller, but not by much, and it is easy to recognise by its black and white plumage. The male has a red nape that is missing in the female. Young great spotted woodpeckers have a red crown. This is the woodpecker that drums. Both sexes drum as a means of stating territory. There is a very distinctive 'tic' call note. Both birds help in excavating the nest hole in which the female lays a clutch of white eggs. Great spotted woodpeckers will enlarge the holes of tit boxes in order to get at whatever is inside, although it is not completely certain if this is to get at the eggs and young of blue tits or to search for insects. To combat this, some bird boxes are produced with metal plates in order to stop the woodpeckers, but here in the Park we have found that this is not really a deterrent. Holes have still been enlarged. Great spotted woodpeckers can drill through metal.

These two woodpeckers are special birds of Christchurch Park. They are distinctive in appearance and we cannot afford to lose them. We have, like the majority of habitats in Suffolk, already lost the lesser spotted woodpecker. Fortunately, this spring has been a particularly good breeding season for both green and spotted woodpeckers so, for the time being, our two woodpeckers are safe.

Sadly, it appears that we no longer have kestrels in the Park either. Kestrel numbers are declining – it is a national trend. Only a few years ago kestrels were very common, with at least two pairs breeding in the Park. A kestrel hovering near the motorway was always a sight to be seen, but not now. Yes, they are still around but in much smaller numbers. It is strange that we now see more hobby falcons and peregrine falcons than we do kestrels. Incidentally, the pair of peregrine falcons that have nested on the Orwell Bridge successfully fledged four young this year, which is amazing.

KESTRELS AND SPARS

There was a time when we had two pairs of kestrels nesting in our Park – now we have none! A pair attempted to nest last year but failed. The RSPB is concerned over the decline of our commonest bird of prey and so they should be. Once again, modern farming methods are blamed. It is pointed out that other farmland birds, such as the grey partridge and corn bunting, are also desperately low on numbers. However, there might be other reasons for the disappearance of the 'windhover'.

When I was a boy, sparrowhawks and kestrels were talked about in the same breath. In our ignorance, we spoke about spars and kestrel hawks, not realising that a kestrel is not a hawk but a falcon. However, the point is that both of these birds were reasonably common. Then the huge reduction in birds of prey in the sixties happened, due to the increased use of pesticides. Subsequently the kestrel did recover its numbers somewhat but the sparrowhawk took much longer, largely because of its persecution by gamekeepers; which brings me to the Wildlife Reserve in Christchurch Park.

For several years now we have known that spars have nested in the tall pines on the edge of the Reserve. Not everyone is enamoured with this bird of prey since, as I have already said, it is a most efficient killer of small birds. This is the bird that will denude your bird table, and maybe even your garden, of your favourite songbirds. Many people are upset to see a sparrowhawk plucking its prey on their linen post or even on their lawn. But let us make one thing absolutely clear – the sparrowhawk is fully protected by law. For those people who are anti, may I suggest that you look more intensely into the life of this spectacular creature? I think we are privileged to have this beautiful bird resident in our Park.

Spars are not the easiest of birds to see when they are nesting. Being secretive is the key to their success, but when they have large young, like all birds of prey, they are extremely noisy. As I write, this year's young have fledged and are airborne for parts of the day, calling most of the time. Malcolm Clark was lucky to see both young and adults in the Park. To witness this, patience is the key. The sparrowhawk therefore is an exciting bird, and the fact that a pair regularly nests in the pines of the Wildlife Reserve makes this area an important habitat. Indeed, a more exciting bird would be difficult to find. During the Friends of Christchurch Park's winter walks led by Philip Murphy, we have occasionally seen spars circling over the Park. The sparrowhawk has rounded wings and a long tail. Closer observation reveals that the male has slate grey upper parts with reddish barred chest. The female is larger and browner. Unlike falcons, which have dark eyes, the sparrowhawk and its larger cousin the goshawk have yellow eyes. Its long legs are also yellow. The female builds the nest of twigs and the eggs number from four to six with our pair usually raising not more than three youngsters. Whilst the female is incubating, the male will bring plucked food to the nest but, when the young are growing fast, both parents will hunt. The female, because of her size, will often take collared and stock doves. The sparrowhawk is a somewhat later nesting bird, with our pair having eggs in late May and the young leaving the nest in July. They stay around the Wildlife Reserve for some weeks before venturing further afield.

It always amazes me that, despite these birds of prey nesting here, they are rarely seen. Yes, of course the fledgling young are noisy as they clamour for food, but when the female is sitting on eggs the pair is silent. There is also very little noise when the male delivers prey. We have all seen these birds outside the breeding season lazily climbing high over the trees, but when delivering food to the nest the male is usually a flash of grey. Love them or hate them, we are privileged to be able to see these birds so close to the town centre. Now that kestrels are no more, we should do all that we can to preserve our beautiful Park and the habitat of the sparrowhawk.

Male sparrowhawk (spar)

SPUDGERS

When I was a young boy, my immediate neighbours had the surnames Nightingale and Sparrow. As far as I can remember, the Nightingales were not very musical and the Sparrows not all that chirpy! I do recall, however, that the member of the Sparrow clan nearest to my age was nicknamed 'Spudger'. Spudger Sparrow! Why do sparrows have that nickname? I do not know, but to me house sparrows have always been 'spudgers'.

Who would have thought that the small house sparrow, so abused in the past, is now revered by the likes of the RSPB? This little bird was so common when I was a boy that sparrow traps were used to reduce its numbers. Spudgers were everywhere, even in the places where no other birds were found. Most of the houses around where I lived had their own population of house sparrows. People who kept birds of prey in those days fed them on sparrows and mice. Nowadays, falconers feed their birds on day-old chicks and rats specially bred for that purpose. Suddenly we have become aware that house sparrows are not nearly as numerous as they once were. In fact, *passer domesticus* is on the red alert list. Whereas in many places sparrows have completely disappeared, here we are a little more fortunate. House sparrows tend to exist in small communities; near the Park there is a pocket of them in Westerfield Road opposite Victoria Nurseries. I hear them chirping away on one side of the road, then see them flying across to the Nurseries to feast on food put out for the ducks. I live close by, but can I get those little spudgers to feed in my garden? No way! I put out birdseed and corn, I put up nest boxes, but to no effect. In recent years I have failed to attract a single spudger into my garden.

House sparrows do come into the Park however, and they can also be found in some of the gardens next to the Park on Westerfield Road. The male sparrow is a smart little fellow, reddish-brown, grey, white and black with a black bib. The only bird it can really be confused with is the tree sparrow, which is an extremely smart-looking bird but slightly smaller than the house sparrow. It has a distinct white wing bar and the crown of its head is chestnut, with no grey as in its relative. A distinguishing feature is its white cheek with a black patch. The bib is black but quite small. Regrettably there are now no tree sparrows in Christchurch Park.

But there is hope. Steve Piotrowski and the Suffolk Wildlife Trust are endeavouring to restore the tree sparrow as a common bird in our county. Much research has been carried out towards this end and, hopefully, Steve and the SWT will be successful. The house sparrow, whilst certainly less common than it used to be, can fortunately still be found in certain areas all over our county. Wouldn't it be wonderful if the tree sparrow population could reach its former numbers, and even better if both species became so numerous that once again we could take them for granted as we did some fifty or sixty years ago. How nice it would be if, instead of saying "gosh look at those sparrows" we simply said "just another flock of spudgers".

There is one other so-called sparrow, the dunnock (known also as the hedge sparrow), which in fact is not a sparrow at all but an 'accentor'. This is a common bird in our Park and it will always be one of my favourites. Why? Well, this bird reminds me of childhood adventures hunting for nests. It builds a beautiful little nest of grass, moss and feathers and lays a clutch of four or five bright blue eggs (in contrast to the off-white, brown spotted eggs of 'real' sparrows). Even back then, I promise, I never called dunnocks spudgers.

"SPUDGERS"

TREE SPARROW
(PASSER MONTANUS)

WHITE CHEEK
AND COLLAR

RED/BROWN CROWN

SMALL BLACK BIB

FEMALE

GREY CROWN

MALE

HOUSE SPARROW
(PASSER DOMESTICUS)

HOUSE SPARROW STILL FOUND
IN AND AROUND PARK IN MUCH
SMALLER NUMBERS THAN IN THE
PAST. TREE SPARROW NO LONGER
FOUND IN PARK.
HEDGE SPARROW (DUNNOCK)
COMMON BIRD OF PARK.

HEDGE SPARROW & NEST
(PRUNELLA MODULARIS)

NOT A SPARROW BUT AN ACCENTOR
USUALLY KNOWN AS A DUNNOCK.
LAYS BLUE EGGS.

REG. SNOOK 2010.

48

HORNETS

When I was a boy, the things we feared even more than adders were wasps, but this didn't stop us lads from trying to destroy their nests. Fighting a wasps' nest was fun – until we got stung. I suppose it was bravado that led us to attack these wasps and it usually ended up with one of us running away, being chased by a swarm of angry 'vespas'. However, hornets were a different kettle of fish. We always steered clear of hornets. We feared these insects because, after all, "three stings from a hornet and you are dead!" Of course, that statement is untrue unless you are allergic to stings, when a single sting might be enough. But, being very young and ignorant of these things, we believed the story and thus left hornets alone. We did find hornets' nests though, since being as mad-keen on bird nesting as we were, it was inevitable that some hole in a tree would hold hornets rather than tawny owls or woodpeckers. Luckily, hornets are obvious insects because they are very slow. You can hear them coming a mile away, and I don't think that their eyesight is all that clever.

Like many insects, the hornet (*vespa crabro*) is having a hard time and it is extremely rare in many places in Britain. I have searched Christchurch Park in vain for hornets – but there must be some. However, I do know where there is a nest. My studio at Grundisburgh is a wooden structure (formerly a cowshed – please don't laugh!) and three feet from my front door and at eye level is a hole the size of a 50p coin. This is the entrance to a hornets' nest. I have lived with this dangerous situation since April of this year and have seen the hornets' numbers increase from about four to perhaps a hundred or more. Only two people have been stung so far (I told them not to put their noses too close to the entrance of the nest!). Luckily, the pain of the sting disappeared fairly quickly and, as yet, I haven't been sued! Certainly, it has been an education to observe this nest at close quarters. I rapidly became used to the droning noise and the sound of chewing from inside the nest cavity. I think hornets have poor eyesight (or else their bodies are too heavy for their wings) since they keep bumping into things – often the watching public. Not once have I seen a hornet fly straight into the entrance hole. Invariably the beast will hit the woodwork and bounce its way to the nest – poor eyesight or what? People have learned not to panic, as this makes hornets frantic and they will gather at the entrance to the nest appearing quite agitated and threatening. On a hot day one or two hornets will stand in the lip of the hole and whirr their wings, presumably to cool the nest.

The hornet's life cycle begins in April when a fertilised female starts to make a nest, often in a dark hollow tree or wall cavity. It builds a series of cells out of chewed bark known as combs, each cell being vertical and sealed at the top. An egg is then laid in the cell and after five to eight days the egg hatches. During this time the queen feeds on a protein-rich diet of insects. The larva builds a silk cap over the cell's opening. During the next two weeks, the larva transforms into an adult (metamorphosis) and eats its way through the silk cap. The first generation of workers, usually females, will then undertake all of the tasks previously carried out by the queen – foraging, nest building and taking care of the brood. However, the egg-laying remains exclusively the duty of the queen. As the colony grows, new combs are made and the cell layers are then enveloped with chewed bark. By late summer there could be 1,000 workers in the colony and the queen starts producing reproductive individuals. Fertilised eggs develop into females called gynes; unfertilised ones develop into males called drones that will not carry out any nest maintenance, foraging or caring of the larvae. In mid autumn the new queens leave the nest and mate during nuptial flights. The males die shortly after mating, and the workers and queens survive until late autumn. Only the fertilised queens will survive the winter.

Surely there are hornets in Christchurch Park. We have many trees with holes in their branches. So please look out for large red, yellow and black wasps buzzing around a tree but view from a distance. Remember, "three stings and ..."

A hornet on a Newton
Wonder apple

ROOKS AND ROACH

When the Suffolk Ornithologists' Group was founded in 1973, the intention was to record the birds of Suffolk in two ways – individual recordings and birds that were found in a particular habitat. Philip Murphy chose to record the birds of Christchurch Park and I was responsible for publishing the SOG bulletin. One of Philip's reports makes for very interesting reading. Rooks ceased to nest in the Park around 1965 but an overnight winter roost of rooks and jackdaws continued here. Philip notes that early one evening in mid-July 1974 about 100 birds were in the trees at the southern end of the Park. They flew off to St Lawrence's Church but quickly returned, soon to be joined by 150 birds that flew in from the north-east. Later, another 2,500 arrived, also from a north-easterly direction. A few days later, the number of roosting rooks and jackdaws amounted to well over 3,000 birds. These corvids were originally part of a huge flock from the Tuddenham area, which would fly to the Park via the trees in the old cemetery. We no longer have a roost of rooks in the Park but Philip's entry does show the importance of note keeping. A huge winter roost of rooks and jackdaws between Tuddenham and Culpho still exists.

Incidentally, there was a report with photos in the national press recently of a pair of red-backed shrikes nesting on Dartmoor, the first time for eighteen years these birds have nested in the UK. As a point of interest, in 1974 a pair of shrikes nested on a piece of waste ground not far from Ipswich town centre and, before that, these birds used to nest on waste ground near St Augustine's Church, the Sidegate Lane allotments, and many other sites nearby (though sadly, not the Park). Ornithologists cannot say for certain why these birds have declined so drastically though it doesn't appear to be a lack of food or nesting sites. However, it may be easier to give a reason for the absence of rooks in our Park. With the town of Ipswich ever expanding, it became nonsense for a roost in Christchurch Park to be situated so far from the rooks' feeding grounds. The huge roost at Tuddenham and Culpho is made up of birds from many different rookeries and on winter afternoons one can see birds approaching from all angles. With these rooks come jackdaws. Why these two birds tolerate each other I do not know. It is strange that when rooks begin to nest – they are very early nesters – their relatives, the jackdaws, seem lost for a while, not really being able to decide whether to go to the original roost or stay with the nesting rooks.

At last we now know something about the fish in the Wilderness Pond. For the last four years since the pond was dredged as part of the Heritage Lottery Project, there has been a yearly hatching of fry. Now the eagle-eyed watcher can see large shoals of various sized fish all of the same species – Roach. Park Manager Sam Pollard and I did a spot of detective work recently and managed to catch two of these fish. We photographed them before releasing them back into the water. Both fish were approximately six inches long and in splendid condition. At the moment we have no fish-eating ducks, only the occasional heron, gull or cormorant, so our fish stocks should continue to grow.

The origin of our fish in the Wilderness Pond is not clear. Some large roach may have remained in the bottom of the pond when it was cleaned out, or possibly placed there unofficially. The chance of fish eggs arriving on the feet of ducks is probably not very large. Many of you will also have noticed the goldfish in the Round Pond. Again, their origin is not clear but the shoals of bright red and gold fish are a sight to behold.

What is brilliant about this is that it shows that both of these ponds are now obviously very healthy and, since the Round Pond has both weed and fish, there is no need for a fountain to oxygenate the water. The pond is beginning to look very attractive, apart from a certain amount of unsightly litter. I don't think we will ever be able to convince people that litterbins are for their rubbish. The Wilderness Pond too always looks beautiful and is a peaceful backdrop to the War Memorial. By being healthy and stocked with so many fish, it really enhances the Wildlife Reserve, but where are the kingfishers?

Roach

Some people confuse roach and rudd as both have red/orange fins and are approximately the same size. However, roach tend to be more silver in colour whereas rudd are more golden. Roach have red eyes, rudd orangey-yellow eyes. Another way of telling the difference is that in roach the front edge of the dorsal fin is above the pelvic fin base; in rudd the dorsal fin starts well behind the pelvic fin base.

MOTHS

Many visitors who have walked through the Wildlife Reserve in Christchurch Park will have noticed that as well as bird boxes there are quite a few bat boxes. These were placed in groups high up on tall trees by our then Park Ranger, Laura. Bats were one of Laura's key interests and her investigations showed that we have at least three species of bat in our Park. I am ashamed to say that my knowledge of bats is poor. Many of the names are unpronounceable (and most of their faces ugly) but if you want to know more about them, then please attend one of the Rangers' summer bat events or look at the Friends of Christchurch Park's excellent website, www:focp.org.uk.

Now, bats feed on flying insects such as moths – so perhaps I can tell you something of these beautiful creatures. In late summer, I rescued an elephant hawk-moth caterpillar that was trying to cross a busy road near to Christchurch Park. If it had not been for me, the crossing would have proved fatal to the caterpillar. As it was, it was nearly fatal for me: despite my vivid description of the beautiful elephant hawk-moth to the irate driver who had applied his brakes to avoid me, he simply muttered "pillock" and drove off. A few days later I came across a garden tiger moth caterpillar which, again, was endeavouring to cross a road. When I was a boy, these caterpillars were so common that I used to collect them in jam jars, but I have not seen a garden tiger moth for ages. It is such a beautiful and striking creature that I really miss seeing them. They are much scarcer and, of course, fly at night, which could be another reason for them eluding me. The forewings are chocolate brown with white markings; the under-wings are usually orange or crimson with black splurges. It is the markings on the forewings that give the garden tiger moth its name, although I think that the markings more closely resemble those of a giraffe rather than a tiger. Perhaps the name 'garden giraffe moth' does not quite have the same ring. This brings me to the emperor moth. Again, when I was very young, part of my haunt was Bixley Heath. Although Bixley Heath is now a nature reserve and monitored by the Ipswich Park Rangers, then the area was much larger and wilder. It was here that I found my first nightjar's nest and where I saw my first adder, caught my first roach and found my first reed warbler's nest (that held a young cuckoo). But it was the emperor moths (*saturnia pavonia*) that I remember so vividly.

As boys we used to look for the caterpillars – large green things with a series of hairy pink pimples on their skin. The emperor moth is the only British species of the silk moth family but the silk it produces is of no commercial use. The larger female moth flies at night and the male flies by day; its antennae can detect the scent of a female from half a mile away. The caterpillars feed on brambles but the cocoon could be found on the stems of the rampant heather that flourished on the heath (before houses were built on it) in July and August. The heather used to grow to three feet or more and we would search the thick stems for the cocoons (chrysalises). Each cocoon was shaped roughly like a gourd used for carrying water, with an opening at one end. A work of art spun in brown silk.

We collected the cocoons and kept them in my mum's airing cupboard where in the spring the beautiful moths would emerge. The female emperor moths were a delicate grey with darker lines and 'eyes', the males were smaller and darker. My parents always ensured that I returned the moths to the heath – probably because my mother objected to sharing her linen cupboard with these large winged insects.

APPLES AND FIELDFARES

A recent initiative by the Park Rangers encouraged people to report old orchards in the Ipswich area. Orchards are rapidly disappearing. In the last ten years we have lost 30% of our apple orchards and 56% of orchards have been grubbed up in the last twenty-five years. Only 29% of apples sold in supermarkets are home grown. Does it matter that we are losing our orchards? Yes, it does. For a start, many of these disappearing orchards had been planted with really old varieties of apple – it would be tragic if these historic fruits were to be lost forever. Many of the gardens near Christchurch Park contain fruit trees and I am certain that many of those are very old.

Adjacent to my studio in Grundisburgh is an ancient orchard containing trees such as greengage, Victoria plum and two pear trees which, despite investigation, remain nameless. Most of the trees, however, are apple trees – old apple trees. One variety is called Monarch. This is a cooking apple raised in 1888 in an orchard in Chelmsford. It is a cross between Peasgood's Nonsuch and Dumelow's Seedling. Another apple found here is Newton Wonder, raised in Derbyshire in 1887. This apple is a cross between Dumelow's Seedling and Blenheim Orange. The third apple is called D'Arcy Spice, raised in 1785 at The Hall, Tolleshunt D'Arcy, Colchester. This remarkable fruit does not ripen until late December or early January when it remains quite small and greenish. It is amazing to see a leafless tree in the New Year covered in apples. The fourth apple in this orchard is a truly great apple, the Blenheim Orange. Raised in Woodstock, Oxfordshire in about 1740, this is a king of apples. It ripens in late autumn, keeps well and tastes delicious.

Now, why am I banging on about apples? The answer is fieldfares (illustrated on the title page of this book). These winter thrushes come to this country in their thousands and the orchard near my studio allows me to watch them gorging on the fallen fruit. They love apples. The fieldfare is a large thrush about the size of a mistle thrush and is usually seen in large flocks. It is a beautiful bird with a grey head and rump, red-brown back and rust coloured breast with heavy spotting. It is told by its chattering call. This is a bird of open fields that feeds on insects and worms as well as apples. In late winter, numbers of this bird will build up on the expansive grassy areas to the north of our Park. A new orchard, Christchurch Orchard, was planted in January 2011 on the hill above the Wildlife Reserve with species that would have grown in East Anglia. The original site of the Mansion's apple orchard lies just to the north of the Park around Victoria Nurseries and a graft of an ancient Ribston Pippin, discovered growing in Stuart Grimwade's garden nearby, is soon to be planted back in the Park in the new orchard.

Two other thrushes pour into our country in the winter – surprisingly, one of those thrushes is the blackbird. Yes, I know the blackbird is here all the year round and is probably our most common thrush, but continental blackbirds hugely reinforce numbers. The other thrush is the delightful redwing. This dainty little thrush comes here to feed on berries, stripping the hedgerows and shrubs of gardens and parks. We see redwings in our Park, especially in the second half of winter when they congregate on the grassy areas near the Westerfield and Park Roads. They are quite tame and allow the onlooker to get very close. These birds are aptly named as they have red colouring under their wings. But perhaps their most distinguishing feature is their prominent white eye-stripe. A delightful bird!

WILDLIFE AND CHRISTCHURCH PARK

C hristchurch Park is a great place to see wildlife. It is also a great place for wildlife itself. But let me suggest that the wildlife would not be so varied if it were not for the gardens around the Park. Obviously, the Soane Street side, facing the town centre, offers less for wildlife, but Westerfield Road, Park Road, Henley Road and the adjacent streets provide a varied habitat for many of Christchurch Park's resident creatures. Nearby houses often have large gardens and these are miniature wildlife reserves in themselves. Some gardens are so close together that they form long corridors that all wildlife, but birds in particular, use as a means of travelling to and from the Park.

Locals are aware that grey squirrels from the Park forage in their gardens, usually to raid bird tables and feeders. Many of us have seen foxes running across the northern end of Christchurch Park, but I wonder how many people know that foxes choose our back gardens in which to rear their young. Certainly, many of us have had foxes 'help' with our gardening. Muntjac can be spotted leaving the Park at dawn and rats are found both in the Park (particularly by the ponds) and in our gardens. Feral cats are often seen prowling along nearby roads, especially at night.

It is birds, however, that benefit most from our gardens. Many of us hang up feeders filled with peanuts or have bird tables where we not only put recommended bird food but also leftovers from meals. The obvious beneficiaries from peanuts and seed are titmice, finches and other small songbirds. But carrion crows and jackdaws soon gobble up the leftovers – all these birds are increasing and commonly seen in the Park. Have you noticed the fat wood pigeons in the Park? Of course you have, and are you aware how daring they are in your garden? Pigeons and doves breed in the Park but I bet the majority breed in our gardens where food is so easily available. Gardening is big business these days – we all like to have shrubs and trees that look pretty and produce attractive berries and fruits – ideal for birds.

In winter, redwings and fieldfares arrive here in large numbers and can be encouraged to feed in our little 'reserves'. And, in recent years, some of us have watched that top winter visitor, the waxwing, feeding on mountain ash berries within feet of our doors. When we dig our gardens, robins, blackbirds and thrushes pounce on what we've uncovered. There is a continual flow of birds from the Park to the nearby gardens, and if you get up early you might see a heron leaving the Wilderness Pond to try its luck in your next door neighbour's fishpond!

Redwings on the upper parkland in winter

TREES

Many Park users have a favourite area, a place of peace and relaxation, be it a small clump of trees, an avenue of limes or, say, a lone, majestic oak. One such tree is the magnificent London plane at the Soane Street entrance to the Park which, from a distance, seems to tower over nearby St Margaret's Church. Even the Wellingtonia in the churchyard cannot compete with this fine specimen.

Our Park is home to many fine oaks. Some are yet to reach maturity, whilst others, previously pollarded, have been there for centuries. The yew by the War Memorial is at least 600 years old. People are fascinated by the gnarled, twisted trunks of the sweet chestnuts near the Reg Driver Centre. Riddled with holes, they provide shelter and nesting sites for many species of wildlife. Perhaps the most iconic view of the Park is the one that greets you from the Westerfield or Park Road entrances: rolling grassland bordered in the distance by a varied collection of beautiful trees.

Most of us also have a favourite time of year for viewing and walking the pathways of Christchurch Park. Even when leafless, a tree is still beautiful. Dark branches clothed in snow or conifers mantled in white are magnificent. But surely springtime is a favourite for many; after a hard winter, to see the horse chestnuts, limes and beeches in their fresh, new livery is simply a joy. As summer arrives, the bright greenery darkens into stronger hues and now shade becomes important, as we – and the Park's wildlife – need shade to shield us from the hoped-for hot summer sun. Finally, autumn approaches, and with it a palette of yellows, reds and browns. If we are fortunate enough to have had a dry, sunny spell, then expect the Park to become a blaze of colour.

WINTER IS WELL AND TRULY HERE!

Walking through Christchurch Park in the first week of December I heard a mistle thrush singing. We are always rushing about these days, so I decided to take time out. I sat on one of the new, beautifully made benches next to the Mansion. The mistle thrush was singing from the top of a lime tree. If you don't know what the song sounds like, then please try and find out because I think you are missing something quite wonderful. The song is gentle and both less loud and staccato than that of the song thrush. It does not fire its song at you. If you listen for it you will surely fall in love with the mistle thrush's song. It does not matter if it is raining; the 'storm-cock' will still perform. Poets have immortalised some birdsong – nightingale, song thrush, cuckoo and even the robin (he that was killed by a sparrow with a bow and arrow) – but few have written about the mistle thrush; Thomas Hardy perhaps ("The darkling thrush"), though we cannot be sure which species he meant.

Whilst sitting there, I noticed that the birds on the Round Pond were very noisy – mallards were quacking and black-headed gulls screeching but, when the noise subsided a bit, the mistle thrush's song could still be heard floating down from the high lime tree.

I have written before about our Mandarin ducks – perhaps the most beautiful of all ducks. I have told you that the Mandarin duck was introduced to this country as an ornamental waterfowl and, because some escaped, wild populations became established. Now they are officially classed as wild British birds. Our population in the Park originated from Victoria Nurseries, about half a mile from the Wilderness Pond, and our birds still fly backwards and forwards between these two places. The ducks use the

Wilderness Pond to preen, display and hopefully nest, but they feed mainly at the Nurseries. Michael, who is in charge of the animals there, feeds the ornamental wildfowl and every day the Mandarins fly up the Westerfield Road, to be fed. Now, the pond at the Nurseries is very small – only about ten or twelve feet across – and it is almost completely covered by trees and shrubs. Yet these ducks do a sort of hovering descent and easily manage to reach the water. They don't call them wood duck for nothing!

I have a friend who has a very ancient apple orchard and a few holly bushes. The grass beneath the apple trees is now strewn with fruit – apart from underneath the Bramley apple trees where the grass is bare. Why is this? Well, fieldfares have arrived and they have scoffed the lot! I don't know why they choose the Bramleys in preference to the others. The holly berries have all gone as well, apart from those on the variegated bush – why? I have not a clue. Mistle thrushes also come to the orchard and, of course, one male is always singing his gentle song from the top of a nearby tree.

I have mentioned before that long-tailed tits have had very good breeding seasons recently – and so have robins. Robins are renowned for singing through the night if there is light from nearby streetlights. So, if you hear birdsong in the very early hours, then it is almost certain to be a robin.

TWITCHERS

Do you know about Twitchers' lists? Twitchers (fanatical bird-watchers) compile all sorts of lists, for example a life list (birds seen during one's lifetime), a year list, a month list, a British list, a county list, and so it goes on. Many birders use New Year's Day as an opportunity to start their year list and on that day there are contests for groups of birders to compete against each other. Occasionally, however, birders are just plain absurd – some armchair birdwatchers have a list of birds they have seen on television. How about that!

But, in my opinion, the most bizarre list I have heard of is one compiled by a dedicated birdman whose Christmas Day list included the following: budgerigar (his own pet), turkey (dead and stuffed), Khaki Campbell duck and chicken (fowl from next door), feral pigeon (from the town centre), three types of pinioned duck in a friend's back garden, a goshawk on a falconer's wrist and a barn owl found dead in the road. Although he was lampooned by many, I suppose he was technically right in saying that they were all birds since they all had feathers (well, apart from the turkey). As for wild birds though, there weren't really any apart from the owl, and that was dead!

Some readers of my notes have remarked that, of all the birds in the Park, I usually seem to be writing about the larger species, ie geese, ducks, crows, etc. Well, I suppose the large birds on the ponds are easy to see, and several members of the crow family are often very prominent on the grassy areas whilst the larger birds of prey can be easily observed overhead. That said, the more proficient observer will know most, if not all, the smaller birds in the Park and will certainly know where to find them.

To a beginner, or less eagle-eyed person, a small brown bird flitting through the undergrowth could be almost anything. However, birdwatching is usually a process of elimination, which becomes easier with more experience. Birdwatchers use the term 'Jizz' which means the way in which a bird behaves, and what a particular species does. With time, even a complete novice can work out that a small brown bird that creeps more closely to the ground is a wren. If that birdwatcher then sees a bird that is definitely not a wren, then the process of elimination has begun. Using gained knowledge to check small birds is not boring, it is exciting. and the best habitat in which to start bird recognition is in your own garden. Check what birds are to be found there, then use that information to find out which birds inhabit another similar environment such as Christchurch Park.

As we look forward to the New Year, we can anticipate what might turn up for us to admire and, of course, an obvious bonanza would be another waxwing invasion. These beautiful northern visitors arrive – often in our gardens – to gorge on berries. So, every day, look out at your berry bushes, cotoneaster, berberis, viburnum or even crab apples. Even if waxwings do not arrive, we can all still look forward to the arrival of spring.

BIRDS LOOKED FANTASTIC IN SNOW
FEEDING ON AN ASSORTMENT
OF BERRIES - INCLUDING MISTLETOE.

FIELD SKETCHES OF WAXWINGS

Waxwings

WE CAN BUT DREAM!

It takes only three or four days of snow and we become totally fed-up with it. Having been spoilt for a number of years with mild winters, it comes as a shock to have to cope with what a few inches of snow involves. Some of us just hibernate! Well, not completely I suppose, but we become reluctant to venture outside of our homes. Whilst others toboggan excitedly down Snow Hill in the Park, we become sedentary, and when the icy weather persists we find it even more difficult to accept. Yes, it looks pretty, but really, a week of 'proper' winter is enough!

So, in these colder days, let's cast our minds back to last summer and perhaps forward to a few months' time. Just think of swallows zooming low over the grassy areas of the Park, swifts screaming overhead or chiffchaffs calling monotonously from the Wildlife Reserve and, with these summer visitors, long hot days that last until about 10pm when night falls at last. No overcoats, wellington boots, scarves, gloves or woollen hats – in fact, very few clothes at all! Barbecues, picnics in the Park or finding shade under our magnificent old oaks and horse chestnut trees. All those halcyon days of midges, wasps and horseflies! But not so very far from Christchurch Park we can also listen to our greatest and most beloved songbird, the nightingale, and perhaps even the cuckoo, though probably no longer the turtle dove. All through the summer our more common birds will be singing their hearts out too. The song thrush will be punching out its tune, competing at times with the lovely mellow tones of the blackbird. Our beloved garden birds will all be looking splendid whilst they busily rear their young, the males serenading us the while with their song. How we miss all this now that the winter is here.

But soon it is New Year! We are heading in the right direction. No matter how long the snow lasts, when it has gone we will soon be looking for signs of spring. Snowdrops will appear, aconites, daffodils and crocuses will follow, then tulips and, before you know it, bluebells. Spring really will be here then, and with the spring our summer visitors will return – house martins, swallows, swifts, warblers and whitethroats and perhaps (but only perhaps) spotted flycatchers.

Despite the snow, the ice and the freezing temperatures of this season, the River Orwell is currently home to great northern divers, mergansers, other northern ducks and large flocks of waders (over 200 snipe were seen recently at nearby Trimley). But when spring does come, the fieldfares, redwings and waxwings will wing their way northwards and our Park will once again be full of birdsong. We can but dream of trees dressed in various shades of green, of the young mallard darting over the Wilderness Pond, of Canada geese and their goslings on the grass, and of huge flocks of painted lady butterflies floating in from Africa…

*Painted ladies
in flight*

BIRD SPECIES OBSERVED IN CHRISTCHURCH PARK

Below is a list of the bird species recorded in, or flying over, Christchurch Park, Ipswich, during the last fifty years. It has been compiled by Philip Murphy from his own observations and those of other reputable ornithologists, and is formatted according to accepted ornithological practice. Ornamental pinioned waterfowl are not included. The record of wrynecks breeding in 1948 was taken from *The Birds of Suffolk* by William H. Payne (1962).

Mute swan
Greylag goose
Canada goose
Brent goose
Shelduck
Carolina duck
Mandarin duck
Mallard
Tufted duck
Pheasant
Little grebe
Cormorant
Grey heron
Sparrowhawk
Common buzzard
Peregrine falcon
Kestrel
Hobby
Moorhen
Oystercatcher
Golden plover
Lapwing
Common snipe
Woodcock

Redshank
Common sandpiper
Black-headed gull
Common gull
Lesser black-backed gull
Herring gull
Common tern
Feral pigeon
Stock dove
Wood pigeon
Collared dove
Turtle dove
Cuckoo
Tawny owl
Swift
Alpine swift
Kingfisher
Wryneck
Green woodpecker
Great spotted woodpecker
Lesser spotted woodpecker
Skylark
Sand martin
Swallow

House martin
Meadow pipit
Yellow wagtail
Grey wagtail
Pied wagtail
Waxwing
Wren
Dunnock
Robin
Black redstart
Wheatear
Ring ouzel
Blackbird
Fieldfare
Song thrush
Redwing
Mistle thrush
Sedge warbler
Reed warbler
Blackcap
Garden warbler
Lesser whitethroat
Common whitethroat
Wood warbler
Chiffchaff
Willow warbler
Goldcrest
Firecrest

Spotted flycatcher
Pied flycatcher
Long-tailed tit
Blue tit
Great tit
Coal tit
Nuthatch
Treecreeper
Jay
Magpie
Jackdaw
Rook
Carrion crow
Starling
House sparrow
Tree sparrow
Chaffinch
Brambling
Greenfinch
Goldfinch
Siskin
Linnet
Redpoll
Common Crossbill
Bullfinch
Hawfinch
Yellowhammer

Alas, many of the species listed above can no longer be seen in Christchurch Park but, as always with birdwatching, one cannot say with certainty that a particular species will not turn up. We can but dream – and keep on looking.

WILDLIFE INDEX

This index does not include the Species List on pages 69-70.
Numbers in bold indicate an illustration.

ABOUT THE AUTHOR

Reg Snook's interest in wildlife was fostered in the years following the Second World War when the countryside was a wonderful place in which a young boy could roam. This led to a lifelong interest in wildlife and a love of birds.

Reg and his family moved to the Christchurch Park area of Ipswich over forty years ago, and since then he has been keeping records of the bird life in the Park. In the late sixties and early seventies, Reg was the local representative of the RSPB for East Suffolk, and as such was privileged to enjoy the friendship of the late Bert Axell, then warden of Minsmere and creator of its 'scrape'. This was an era when there were more coypus than marsh harriers, more red-backed shrikes than bearded tits.

In 1973, Reg was one of the founder members of the Suffolk Ornithologists' Group, which has now grown into perhaps the most important bird-recording group in Suffolk. For the past 29 years (a period when the numbers of birds of prey in the British Isles have increased dramatically), Reg has also worked as a Government Wildlife Inspector specialising in birds of prey. Following the devastating hurricane of October 1987, Reg assisted Mike Stagg, head Park Ranger, in setting up the Bird Reserve in Christchurch Park, the area that is now known as the Wildlife Reserve.

Reg's other main passion is his art. He paints not only the birds and animals he knows so well but, since the millennium, he has completed over 200 portraits of the village people of Grundisburgh. His studio in that village is always open and welcoming to visitors.